KNOWLEDGE ENCYCLOPEDIA
INSECTS

© Wonder House Books 2024

All rights reserved. No part of this book may be reproduced or transmitted in any form by any means, electronic or mechanical, including photocopying and recording, or by any information storage and retrieval system except as may be expressly permitted in writing by the publisher.

(An imprint of Prakash Books)

contact@wonderhousebooks.com

Disclaimer: The information contained in this encyclopedia has been collated with inputs from subject experts. All information contained herein is true to the best of the Publisher's knowledge.

ISBN : 9789354400094

Table of Contents

Creepy Crawlies	3
Spot the Insect	4–5
The Menacing Weevil	6
The Colourful Scarab	7
The Helpful Ladybug	8
The Glowing Firefly	9
Butterfly or Moth?	10–11
Caterpillars Get Wings	12
The Migratory Monarch	13
Jump and Chirp	14–15
The Mighty Dragonfly	16–17
The Praying Mantis	18
The Hidden Sticks	19
A Historical Pest	20
Unwelcome House Guests	21
The Busy Bee	22–23
The Useful Bee	24
The Silk Road	25
The Builder Ants	26–27
The Active Termites	28–29
The Dangerous Mosquito	30
The Irksome Housefly	31
Word Check	32

CREEPY CRAWLIES

Think about all the insects that you see around you. Did you know that some are only found in tropical forests? There also exist poisonous insects, insects that have six legs, and even insects that can fly. Around a million insect species have already been discovered, but scientists estimate that there might be many many more out there. Insects are extremely varied and exist in large numbers. It is estimated that for every human on the planet, we have 1.4 billion insects to match.

They are a group so diverse and widely spread out that they cover all the nooks and crevices of the world, from the Arctic snow to desert rocks, and from deep oceans to hot springs. In fact, a single swarm of desert locusts can cover an area of 1,200 square kilometres and contains close to 80 million insects. No wonder they are a part of our daily lives. Read on to learn about the interesting world of insects.

▼ The butterfly too is an insect. It transforms from a caterpillar and sprouts those colourful wings

Spot the Insect

Insects account for almost 80 per cent of the animal species in the world. Now that is a huge number! All of these insects belong to the larger group of invertebrate animals known as **arthropods**. This is the same group to which scorpions, spiders, crabs, and lobsters belong.

Body

An adult insect found anywhere in the world has three common body parts—head, thorax, and abdomen. Most insects have three pairs of legs, two pairs of wings, and two antennae. The eyes, mouth, and antennae are on the head; the legs and wings are attached to the thorax. The abdomen has most of the organs, such as the stomach and intestine.

▼ *The jewel beetle is one of the most colourful insects in the world, belonging to order Coleoptera*

Exoskeleton

Insects are covered with a hard exoskeleton made up of chitin, which contains proteins and carbohydrates. In an insect, the eyes are covered with a thin layer of exoskeleton. This is a non-living structure; hence it does not grow with the insect. At every stage of growth, the insect moults.

Moulting refers to the process by which the exoskeleton is shed to regrow a new one. At this point of time the insect, with its soft exterior, is most vulnerable to predators and its surrounding environment. Many insects go into hiding until the tough, new exoskeleton grows back.

Apart from protection, the exoskeleton of the insect gives its body shape and prevents it from drying. It has tiny holes called **spiracles**. These are small openings or pores that allow respiration. The exoskeleton is made up of varied patterns and colours. Bright colours warn the predators that the insect is poisonous, while dull colours make for good camouflage.

◀ *A cicada shedding its exoskeleton while entering the next stage of its life*

Classification

All insects belong to the class Insecta. They are classified into several groups. Most of the insects on our planet belong to the following orders—Coleoptera (scarabs and beetles), Lepidoptera (butterflies and moths), Hymenoptera (ants, wasps, and bees), and Diptera (flies or 'true' flies).

There are many species of insects belonging to each of these classes. 40 per cent of the known species of insects belong to order Coleoptera. The order Lepidoptera has about 180,000 species of insects. Order Hymenoptera has about 115,000 known species, while around 125,000 species belong to order Diptera.

Sense-able

Insects have a good sense of touch, smell, hearing, and sight. They do not have ears, but their skin can pick up sound waves. For a few insects such as grasshoppers and crickets, the tympanal organ acts like the ears. Insects use their antennae to feel and smell. They need to have a keen sense of smell to detect food and mates.

Eyesight

Insect eyes can detect movement but cannot see shapes as we do. Not all insects can see colours, but few, such as butterflies have exceptional vision to find flowers.

Insects can have two types of eyes; each species might have either of the types or both. The first type are called the ocelli. These are simple, small eyes. They cannot see well but can detect dark and light. These eyes are seen on insects like fleas.

The second type are huge, bulging eyes like that of the housefly. These are called compound eyes. They are made up of many tiny single eyes. Each single eye is called the ommatidium. It sees its own image and sends it to the insect brain. The brain then combines all the images to form a bigger picture.

▲ Wasps and ants have both types of eyes

Of Legs and Joints

The word 'arthropod' means to have jointed feet. Insects are arthropods, which means their legs have joints just like the joints on human legs. However, their legs do not have bones inside them; they have muscles instead. These muscles allow the insects to move, bend, run, and jump.

One of the fastest insects in the world is the Australian tiger beetle. It cannot fly but can run at a speed of 9 kmph. Another fast insect is the tiger moth caterpillar which picks up a speed of 5 kmph.

Wings

Insect wings are made up of chitin. The muscles attached to the exoskeleton make these wings flap. Most insects such as bees, beetles, and dragonflies have two pairs. Insect wings are thin and transparent, but veins running between them make them sturdy.

▲ A species of grasshopper called tropidacris cristata

This is not to say that all insects have wings. Remember, there is great diversity in the insect world. Fleas, lice, and bedbugs, for example, are wingless. Few insects such as aphids can even grow wings whenever needed, such as in the case of food shortage or overcrowding. At such times, the insects need wings to fly away to a better place. Aphids are commonly called greenflies and blackflies. Many aphid species choose to feed on only one type of plant for their entire lives. So, they are called **monophagous**.

Isn't It Amazing!

Cicadas are among the loudest insects in the world. They have special organs called tymbals that produce their characteristic sounds which can sometimes reach 90 decibels! This is as loud as the sound produced by a motorcycle.

The Menacing Weevil

Beetles and weevils belong to the order Coleoptera. This order has close to 350,000 insect species. Coleoptera is not just the largest insect order, but also the largest group of animals in the world. The number of insects classified within this order is rising each year with the discovery of new species by scientists. Coleopterans are seen in almost all habitats of the world, right from oceans, mountains, and deserts to cold regions.

Colourful Beetles

The word 'Coleoptera' comes from the Greek words, '*koleos*' or sheath and '*pteron*' or wings. This refers to the special arrangements of wings in beetles. Similar to other insects, beetles have two pairs of wings. However, one pair is slightly modified.

The front wings in these beetles are hard and strong. They cover the upper side of the body like a sheath. This hard casing-like structure is called the **elytra**. Elytra protect the delicate rear wings. The rear wings are folded under the elytra at rest, but when the beetle is about to fly, they emerge from the casing.

▲ Beetles exist in different colours. This is the spotted cucumber beetle

Weevils

There are about 40,000 species of weevils in existence in the world. Most species are brown or grey, but the diamond beetle is colourful. Weevils are also called snout beetles because they have long, curved snouts which look like elephant trunks. The snouts are used to make holes in leaves to lay eggs. They are also used to penetrate the leaves.

Most weevils have long foldable antennae. These antennae fold into special grooves present on the snout. They are small animals, measuring about 6 millimetres; but there are exceptions with few measuring almost up to 7–8 centimetres. Weevils feed on fruits, stems, flowers, and seeds.

▲ Weevils have managed to survive because of their snouts

Into the Grain

Grain weevils are small brown weevils, not more than 4 millimetres long. They make the most menacing pests as they destroy stored grain such as maize, oats, and wheat. The females bore holes in individual grains to lay eggs. The larvae, which emerge from these eggs, feed on the grain. When they are threatened, they feign death. This is how they protect themselves from predators.

Cotton Soft

The boll weevil is about 6 millimetres in length. But it makes for a terrible guest, as it enjoys destroying its host—the cotton bolls. The female boll weevil lays eggs in cotton buds. The larvae from the eggs feed on the cotton seeds as well as fibres, completely destroying them. Farmers have to bear immense losses every year because of the boll weevils.

▲ Grain weevils are also known as wheat weevils

▲ Boll weevils cannot feed or breed on any plant other than cotton

The Colourful Scarab

Scarabs are a big family of beetles comprising more than 30,000 species. That means that 10 per cent of all known beetles are actually scarabs! The sacred scarab is one of the most famous members of the scarab family. In ancient Egypt, it was worshipped as the incarnation of the Sun god Khepri. Various species of scarabs are found all around the world, except for Antarctica and the oceans.

Appearance

Scarabs are usually black or brown in colour, but there exist species which are mesmerising with bright colours, beautiful patterns, and metallic sheens. They are oval in shape with stout bodies. Sizes could vary with the smallest being just about 2 millimetres and the largest being around 17 centimetres.

An interesting feature of the scarabs is the presence of special antennae on their bulky bodies. The ends of the antennae are made up of three flat plate-like structures which form a club. Their front legs allow them to freely dig in the mud because of their toothed edges.

▲ *This insect with a seemingly metallic sheen belongs to a species of beetle called Protaetia*

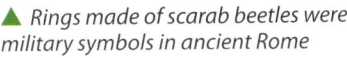
▲ *Rings made of scarab beetles were military symbols in ancient Rome*

Diet

Scarabs have a varied diet. Some species eat fruits, insects, as well as carrion, while others eat the slime of snails. Some, like the Japanese beetles, are pests. Did you know that a large group of Japanese beetles can eat the leaves and fruits of a peach tree within a few minutes, leaving only the branches behind?

Incredible Individuals

In Egyptian mythology, all the main gods acquired the characteristics of creator gods. A single figure could have many names; among those of the Sun god, the most important were Khepri (the morning form), Re-Harakhty (a form of Re associated with Horus), and Atum (the old, evening form). Khepri was associated with the scarab beetle because the ancient Egyptians associated the insect rolling a ball of dung on the floor with the invisible forces that contributed to the movements of the Sun in the sky.

Dung Beetles

Dung beetles come in varieties called rollers, tunnellers, and dwellers, depending upon how they treat the dung. Rollers simply make dung balls which they roll away and store in a safe place to consume later or use the balls to lay eggs. On the other hand, the dwellers use the dung as their home. Females lay their eggs in the dung and when the larvae emerge, they have food to eat. The tunnellers create a tunnel underneath the waste material.

▲ *Dung beetles can roll up to 1,141 times their weight, which is why they are the strongest insect in the world*

The Helpful Ladybug

The ladybug is a small, beautiful insect with a shiny red and black body bearing seven black spots. There are 5,000 species of these insects, but the red-and-black spotted ladybug is the most famous. Ladybugs belong to the beetle family. They are also known as ladybirds or lady beetles. Read on to find out how the insect got this interesting name.

▲ The spots on ladybugs are meant to warn attackers that these beetles taste terrible

▲ Ladybugs pose no threat to human beings

Behaviour

Ladybugs are found in varied habitats. They live in forests, grasslands, cities, and even on farms. In cold weather they **hibernate** in rocks, farm homes, or logs.

These tiny creatures are oval with a dome-shaped structure on their backs and tiny legs. They come in various colours such as red, orange, yellow, black, and pink. These colours serve as a warning to the predators. If ladybugs feel threatened, they release a foul-smelling liquid from the joints in their legs. They are also known to play dead at times in the presence of a predator. Adult females lay eggs near insect colonies. Once the larvae emerge, the first thing they do is eat. The form and behaviour of beetles, even the ladybugs, have inspired many inventions among people. The car manufacturer Volkswagen created a car inspired by and named after beetles.

A Holy Name

Ladybugs are not just good to look at; they are also very useful to farmers as they devour aphids and other insects which can harm their crops. A single ladybug can eat close to 5,000 insects in its lifetime. That is a lot for such a small creature.

Long ago in Europe, farmers were being harassed by crop-eating insects. They began to pray to the Virgin Mary for help. Then they realised that there was one insect which helped them eat up these pests; it was the ladybug. As a thanks to the Virgin Mary for saving their crops, they called the insect 'beetle of our Lady'. As the years passed, the name changed to ladybug. However, not all ladybugs are nice to crops. The Mexican bean beetle, a species of the ladybug, eats the bean plant, while the squash beetle eats the squash plant.

▲ A Mexican bean beetle prefers the beans growing on a bean plant as its host

In Real Life

Beetles hate salt water. But some species love fresh water. The diving beetles use their hairy legs as oars to wade in the water. Of course, they have to come to the surface every few minutes to gulp in air. The Namib Desert beetle is a species that lives in the deserts of Africa, where water is sparse. It survives in the desert by harvesting moisture from the air, condensing it on its back and storing the water. This has inspired human beings to conserve water using innovative techniques.

The Glowing Firefly

Fireflies can glow. On hot summer nights, if you step outside, especially where there is quiet and peace, you might find a mild, intermittent glow coming from some trees. Deep in the forests these glows are aplenty. The source is the firefly, a type of beetle. There are about 2,000 known species of fireflies in the world.

▲ *The light shows of fireflies are mating acts*

What are Fireflies?

Fireflies are soft-bodied beetles, about 2.5 centimetres long. They are black or brown in colour with yellow or orange markings. Most fireflies are nocturnal insects, but there are some species which are diurnal. That means some fireflies are active in the day and night. Adult fireflies survive on pollen and nectar, while there are also some which do not eat at all. In a few cases, the female of one species targets the male from another as prey. Fireflies love warmth, which is why they are a common occurrence in the humid regions of Asia and North America. They are found in the temperate belt near damp places.

Glow in the Dark

The glow of the fireflies comes from an organ located underneath their abdomen. In the organs are special cells which carry a substance called luciferin. The fireflies take in oxygen and combine it with luciferin to produce their characteristic glow. Scientifically, the glow is called **bioluminescence**, which means the production of light by a living organism.

The luminescence of fireflies is specific to species. Scientists still have to unravel the mystery of the intermittent glowing patterns displayed by these insects. So far, we know that the light is emitted to not just attract potential mates but also to warn a predator to keep away.

▲ *Some species of fireflies synchronize their flashing*

Glow Worms

Females lay eggs in the ground. After the incubation period, the larvae emerge from the eggs and are called glow worms. This is because even the larva of a firefly can emit a glow. The larvae live on the ground, feeding on snails, slugs, and some other types of worms. Before eating, the larvae inject a sort of numbing fluid into the prey.

Finding Fireflies

People can see fireflies in the jungles of Southeast Asia, especially Thailand, Malaysia, Philippines, China, and India. People from these places have reported seeing 'the dance of the fireflies'. In USA, the insects put up a great show at the Great Smoky Mountain National Park. Fireflies are also found in abundance in the humid rainforests of Central and South America, and parts of Australia. Remember to be quiet when you want to see their beautiful glow.

Isn't It Amazing!

The African Goliath beetle is named after the biblical giant Goliath. No wonder, because this is one of the heaviest insects in the world. It weighs close to 100 grams.

Butterfly or Moth?

Butterflies and moths belong to order Lepidoptera, whose name means 'scaly wings'. The large, thin wings of these insects are covered with tiny scales. Along with the wings, the body and legs too are covered with scales, which come off if the insects are held. The order Lepidoptera is the biggest family of insects after Coleoptera. It consists of almost 180,000 species.

Similar but Different

There is a reason that butterflies and moths look similar—they are cousins! However, they have many differences which make it easy to tell them apart. There are 20,000 species of butterflies, but there are a whopping 160,000 species of moths. While butterflies are active during the day, moths are active during the night. Butterflies sport bright and beautiful colours. But moths often have dull brown or grey patterns on their wings. Butterflies have club-like antennae, while moths have feathery antennae.

An interesting thing about these insects is that when butterflies are at rest, they hold their wings vertically in place. But moths have a variety of ways to hold their wings. They hold their wings like a tent above their bodies, or spread them out horizontally, and even wrap them around their bodies.

Sweet Nectar

What do butterflies and moths feed on? They eat the nectar produced in flowers. Nectar is a food source containing lots of energy-rich sugars. Butterflies and moths eat nectar when they become adults as they need lots of energy to fly. In tropical forests, nectar is available all year. However, in cold regions, flower production is seasonal, so butterflies and moths have a corresponding life cycle.

Butterflies and moths have a unique ability not seen in other insects. They can coil up their proboscis or feeding tube. To sip nectar from deep in the flower, the feeding tube becomes straight. It is used like a straw to suck out the sweet substance.

Apart from nectar, few species are also known to feed on mosses, lichens, ferns and even grains. The flour moth is one such insect, it devours stored grains and cereals. The fungus moth and scavenger moth feed on decaying and dead plant remains.

◀ *Butterflies actually have four wings, not two*

▶ *Butterflies come in various colours and patterns. Several of them hide from predators using their colourful wings*

Usefulness

Lepidopterans have made homes in all continents except Antarctica. They live in forests, grasslands, mountains, deserts, and even cities. Due to their various hues and patterns, butterflies are considered to be beautiful and are captured in art by humans. They have served as inspiration in designing jewellery and decorative ornaments as well as in the clothing industry.

Lepidopterans have been used to study the environment as well as changes in the climate. They also help the country benefit monetarily as butterfly parks and tours have been set up in many parts of the world. Tourists take these up in hordes.

Butterflies and moths are important **cross pollinators**. For example, the South American cactus moth has been introduced in Australia to clear out hectares and hectares of prickly pear cactus, a weed harmful to crops.

In Real Life

Moths are nocturnal insects. They are attracted to light because of a phenomenon called phototaxis. The movement of their wings is influenced by the strength of light. With distant sources of light, such as the Moon, the light reaches equally to both eyes, thereby causing the insect to fly in a straight line. But if the source of light is closer, such as a candle flame or electric bulb, the moth perceives it strongly in one eye rather than in both eyes. As a result, the wings on one side are stimulated to move faster, causing the insect to fly right into the light source.

▲ *Many adult moths don't eat*

ANIMALS | INSECTS

 Trivia

The peacock butterfly has a special pattern on its wings that looks like eyes. It uses these eyespots to scare and ward off predators.

The purple bog fritillary is a polar insect living in cold temperatures all through the year. These butterflies have dark and hairy bodies to absorb more heat. They are smaller than the average butterfly so that they can warm up quickly.

◀ The peacock butterfly has eye-shaped patterns on its wings. It sits in a way that the eyes become prominent, scaring away its predators

▲ The patterns on the underside of the purple bog fritillary butterflies are lighter than their dorsal or upper side patterns

The western spruce budworm moth mainly consumes needles of fir and spruce. But the larvae of this moth are devastating pests affecting the coniferous forests of the USA and Canada. Infestation densities as low as 15–20 caterpillars per square metre can lead to rapid **defoliation** and further death of the trees.

The sunset moth found in Madagascar is often mistaken for a butterfly. This is because it is active during the day and has colourful patterns on its wings. It is considered to be one of the world's most beautiful insects.

▲ The flashy colours of the sunset moth are created by the curvature of the scales on their wings that reflect light in different angles

◀ The giant swallowtail butterfly feeding on a pink zinnia flower. They are some of the largest butterflies found in North America.

▼ Butterflies are attracted to specific types and colours of flowers

Caterpillars Get Wings

A life cycle refers to the changes an organism goes through after it is born until it reaches adulthood. Some organisms, which include butterflies and moths, undergo a process called **metamorphosis**, which means that they go through so many drastic changes that they look completely different as adults than when they were newborns.

01 Egg

First, the male and female butterflies or moths have to find each other. They do so in varied ways. In cecropia moths, at mating time, females produce natural chemicals which are smelled by the males almost 2 kilometres away. The males use their feathery antennae to detect the smell. Once the male and female of the species mate, the female is ready to lay eggs.

The female butterfly or moth lays eggs on the underside of leaves or on stems. Usually, the eggs are laid on plants which are eaten by the new hatchlings, so that they do not have to go hunting for food. For example, the female brimstone butterfly lays eggs on buckthorn leaves. During the next stage, the caterpillars eat these leaves.

04 Butterfly or Moth

At last, the butterfly or moth is ready inside the pupa. The pupa breaks open, but the adult does not fly immediately. Its wings are still wet, wrinkled, and stuck to the body. The butterfly or moth waits for them to dry. To make them strong, the insect pumps a fluid called haemolymph into them. Once the wings are ready for flight, the butterfly or moth takes off.

▲ The life cycle of a butterfly

▲ Moths are one of the largest pollinator groups besides bees and butterflies

◀ Butterfly emerging from pupa

03 Pupa

The caterpillar's next phase is not to be a moth or butterfly, but to change into an inactive, hard-cased pupa or chrysalis. It attaches itself to stems or twigs of plants. This stage lasts for days, even weeks depending upon the species. The hard case protects the budding butterfly inside from predators and extreme weather conditions. The caterpillar starts to develop legs, wings, and other organs that will make it a butterfly or moth.

This stage of the insect's life is quite crucial as it is essentially defenceless. Lots of caterpillars do not reach the next stage due to attacks from predators or other challenges such as harsh weather.

02 Caterpillar

The eggs hatch and the caterpillars emerge. As soon as they are born, they start eating a lot. During this phase, caterpillars moult several times. As a caterpillar grows its skin gets tighter and splits or cracks appear on the surface. After emerging from the egg, a caterpillar can grow up to 100 times its size. It is now ready for the next stage.

◀ Caterpillars feed on plants such as cudweed, tulips, and black cherries

The Migratory Monarch

The regal-sounding monarch butterfly is an interesting insect. Not only does it migrate, but it also has an effective self-defence mechanism. The butterfly uses a chemical defence system. At the caterpillar stage, it eats milkweed plants, which contain toxic compounds called cardenolides. The toxins accumulate in its body, protecting it and subsequently the adult monarch from predators.

Appearance

The monarch is a stunning butterfly with orange wings marked with black veins and borders, and white spots. The wingspan of an adult monarch could be close to 12 centimetres. Between the male and female monarch butterflies, it is the females which have thicker veins on their wings. The colourful scheme helps ward off the predators.

Migration

Monarchs are not native to only Central, North, and South America, but are also found in Australia, India, parts of Europe, and some islands in the Pacific Ocean. The interesting thing about monarchs is that this migration is practiced only by the North American butterflies. Just before winter every year, hordes of these tiny butterflies get ready for migration. They leave their summer breeding grounds in the USA and Canada to travel more than 5,600 kilometres to reach southern California and central Mexico. It is said that millions of butterflies are a part of the migration. Most monarch butterflies return to the same woodland.

▲ A monarch butterfly resting on a flower

Under Threat

Since 1983, the International Union for Conservation of Nature (IUCN), a body that governs all animal and plant species around the world, has listed the monarch butterfly's migration as threatened. In Mexico, huge tracts of land, where these butterflies used to make their homes, were cleared of forests and replaced with plantations. Also, milkweed trees are reducing in number because of logging.

Unsolved Mystery

Monarchs survive for a few months. Towards the end of winter, the male and female monarchs in Mexico and California mate. The males die and females head northwards. On the way, they lay eggs on the milkweed trees and die. How the next generation knows where to go is still an enigma. The butterflies might have an internal compass that helps them reach the right place in the right season.

ⓘ Incredible Individuals

A zoologist named Fred Urquhart (1911–2002) discovered where the monarch butterflies spent their winters in 1975. After his findings were published in the National Geographic, the government of Mexico demarcated certain areas in the country for the protection and conservation of these butterflies in 1979. However, Fred Urquhart started doing his research in 1937 and only completed it 38 years later. He worked with his wife, Norah Roden Urquhart, who tracked and tagged several butterflies for their research. He discovered several other facts about butterflies during his research. According to Urquhart, butterflies only take flight during the day, when there is sunlight. They can fly 130 kilometres in one day. Butterflies of all ages from different generations fly together during the migration period.

◀ Scientists are yet to unravel the mystery of the monarch migration

Jump and Chirp

Crickets and grasshoppers belong to the insect order Orthoptera. This is the same order that dragonflies, stoneflies, and cockroaches belong to. Most of these insects have the ability to camouflage so that they can blend into their surroundings.

The Hind Wonder

Have you ever tried to touch a grasshopper? If you have, you must have noticed the leaps it takes. Both crickets and grasshoppers have powerful hindlegs for leaping and jumping, usually to escape predators. As they leap, they spread their rear wings. The rear wings are larger, with a membrane, and are usually colourful. Both the insects have rigid forewings.

The Ear Tale

Grasshoppers and crickets have no ears. Instead they both have an organ—a stretched membrane of skin—called the tympanum. In case of crickets, it is located on the knee-like joints of their front legs, while in grasshoppers the membrane is located underneath the abdomen. The organ detects sound vibrations which are sent to the brain.

Sing a Song

The chirping of crickets and grasshoppers is a very familiar sound in summers, especially in cold regions. The noise created is not actual singing but is called **stridulating**. It is created by rubbing two body parts together. Crickets rub their front wings to create the sound, while grasshoppers rub their hindlegs against the front wings. Most often, the male insects sing. They do so to warn others off their territory or to attract mates.

▼ *Grasshoppers existed long before dinosaurs*

Wings

Spiracles

Hindleg

Midleg

▲ *Crickets have more protein than beef or salmon*

◄ *Most grasshoppers have a herbivorous diet*

Katydids are a species of crickets. They make sounds just like crickets and grasshoppers. While the songs of most crickets get repetitive within a second, the song of katydids repeats in an alternating pattern. Different species also have their own songs. The US katydids are called virtuoso katydids for this reason. However, they perform at a high frequency, so people might not be able to hear their songs.

Amplified

The mole cricket is an interesting insect. Male mole crickets make special burrows during mating season. They dig two trumpet-shaped openings which act as megaphones. It is through these loudspeakers that they send across their mating calls. On a still night, these calls can be heard from almost 400 metres away.

 ## On Hatching

The young **nymphs**, as they are called, of the grasshoppers and crickets look like smaller versions of the adults, except they lack wings. As the nymphs grow and shed their skin, the wings emerge slowly. With each successive moult the nymph resembles an adult more and more. This type of development, where there is no pupa stage, is called **incomplete metamorphosis**.

Crickets v/s Grasshoppers

Crickets and grasshoppers have certain dissimilarities which make it easy to tell them apart. Crickets have long antennae, while grasshoppers have short antennae. Crickets come out at dusk, but grasshoppers are active during the day. Crickets do not eat plants, but they can eat animals and each other. On the other hand, grasshoppers strictly rely on plants for food. An earwig is a small herbivorous, nocturnal insect belonging to the same family as the grasshoppers and crickets. It sprays a foul-smelling liquid to defend itself from predators, but it is harmless to us.

 ## Mating

The perfect time to find mates is during summer, when the weather is warm. Grasshoppers and crickets turn to their musical abilities for this. Soon they get a mate to create the new generation. Most often, the adult insects in both types do not last the harsh winters, especially in colder climatic regions. It is only their eggs which survive the cold. However, in warmer regions the insects tend to survive longer.

 ## Securing the Eggs

Female grasshoppers dig a hole in the ground, pushing the abdomen hard to release anywhere between 20–100 eggs. The eggs are covered with a white frothy liquid which solidifies to form a casing. It is this casing and the soil that protects the eggs throughout winter. Once the incubation period is over, tiny grasshoppers emerge from the eggs.

In case of crickets, the story is slightly different. Similar to the grasshoppers, female crickets dig holes in the soil, but here the female digs as many holes as the eggs she lays. The number of eggs is usually 100 and a single hole has a single egg. The eggs are protected by the soil in winters. After incubation, tiny crickets emerge from the eggs.

▲ *A grasshopper carefully laying eggs*

 ## Incredible Individuals

Dr William H. Cade is a biologist who conducted research on field crickets and flies, as well as the evolution and reproduction habits of insects. He studied the acoustic signals of a cricket and the mating habits of cockroaches. In 1975, he made a discovery with his wife, Elsa Salazar Cade. They found that a female **parasitic** fly actually becomes attracted to the male cricket's song. They deposit larvae near these males. The larvae eat up the crickets within a week and enter the pupa stage. So, he discovered that these parasitic flies are the natural enemies of crickets.

The Mighty Dragonfly

Dragonflies are also called the devil's darning needle. They belong to the Odonata order of insects, which in Greek means the 'toothed one'. Yes, a dragonfly is known for its saw-like teeth. These insects have been around for almost 300 million years, but they have not changed much from their ancestors.

Tracing the Evolution

Insects first appeared about 380 million years ago at a time called the Devonian Period. They were small and wingless, without any developed legs. The next stage in evolution was the development of wings. The oldest fossil evidence dates back to the Carboniferous Period, which was 300 million years ago. It was then that the first dragonflies appeared. It is said that dragonflies grew to monstrous proportions, with a wingspan of almost two feet, as much as any modern bird.

▲ Dragonflies reproduce by indirect insemination

Modern Dragonflies

As they evolved, the dragonfly's wing size reduced to 2–15 centimetres, which is the same as the modern dragonfly. The wings are delicate, veined, and generally transparent with coloured markings. The dragonfly's body is long. The insect has two pairs of wings, one in the front and another in the back. Both the wing pairs are shaped differently. At rest, the wings do not fold close to the body but are spread out. Dragonflies have compound eyes that give them 360° vision to spot their prey as well as their predator.

▲ The dragonfly is small, but it has many complex parts

👤 In Real Life

Do you know there roamed cockroaches three or four times as big as those present today? This happened during the Carboniferous Period. It is said that abundant swamps and forests created excess oxygen in the atmosphere. Oxygen, although an essential gas for survival, can lead to harmful effects if inhaled in excess. Small bugs could not have sustained the excess gas, so scientists theorise that they grew in size, in proportion to the amount of oxygen their bodies could take in for survival.

Flight of the Dragon

Dragonflies are experts in flying. They can move up, down, backwards, sideways, or hover like a helicopter. The interesting thing about this insect is that it usually catches its prey in mid-air. Small flying insects such as mosquitoes, bees, and butterflies are easy prey. Dragonflies have not changed their ancient flying technique. Their wings are controlled directly by their muscles. These sets of muscles contract and relax alternately, which pulls the wings up and down.

▲ There are more than 5,000 known species of dragonflies

Optimum Requirement

The muscles of dragonflies have to reach an optimum temperature before flight. Small dragonflies can take off with a body temperature of 12°C, but larger ones need a minimum temperature of 20°C. To reach these temperatures, the insects bask in the heat of the Sun or engage in rapid movement of their wings. If the insect overheats, it glides in the air to cool down.

A Family Affair

Dragonflies can reach a speed of almost 97 kmph. The globe skimmer, a migratory dragonfly, is known to make an annual multigenerational journey of almost 18,000 kilometres. This means that generations of dragonflies take the journey together. On the way, the younger dragonflies breed, and the older generations die out.

▶ Despite having six legs, most dragonflies can barely walk

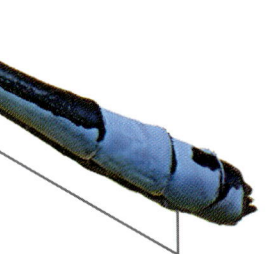

Isn't It Amazing!

The other name of the dragonflies, the devil's darning needle, comes from an old superstition. It was believed that these insects could sew up the mouth, eyes, and ears of sleeping children, especially, those who misbehaved. In reality, the dragonfly is harmless to human beings. In fact, human beings pose a bigger threat to their survival due to climate change.

▲ Dragonflies can see even ultraviolet and polarized light

Generation Next

Dragonflies live in areas with abundant water. First comes the egg stage. The female of the species lays the eggs in plant tissue, moist soil, and in water or on its surface. Depending on the incubation time of the dragonfly species (there exist close to 5,000 species of dragonflies in the world), the eggs hatch. The newly emerged nymph leads an aquatic existence. It is a voracious eater, preying on small fish, crustaceans, tadpoles, and worms.

The nymphs get oxygen through their gills located at the end of the digestive canal. Expanding and contracting their bodies, they force water through the gills. They swim in the same way, using the force of water. Depending on the species, the larvae moult a number of times. Eventually, they become beautiful adult dragonflies; these can lead an adult life spanning between 4 months to 10 years.

The Praying Mantis

The praying mantis, also known as *Mantis religiosa*, is a small but fierce hunter. It is known to take on animals much larger than its own size.

What's in a Name?

The praying mantis gets its name because of its long front legs. They are bent such that the mantis seems to be kneeling in prayer. This insect belongs to a bigger group of hunters called the mantids. Over 2,400 species species of mantids exist in the world.

Waiting for Prey

The praying mantis has a triangular head on which are perched two large compound eyes and three smaller simple ones between them. These eyes have blessed the insect with excellent vision. With its long neck, the insect can turn its head 180° to scan the surroundings.

While sitting on leaves, it is camouflaged properly because of its bright green colour. As it rests between the flowers and branches of a plant, the praying mantis waits for hours for its prey to appear. Once the prey comes closer, the praying mantis strikes with lightning speed and grabs the prey with its pincer-like spiny front legs. The rest of the four legs are used for walking.

Diet

The praying mantis is known to eat moths, crickets, and grasshoppers. Occasionally, it is known to eat very small birds such as hummingbirds and even reptiles. In Karnataka, India, a team of scientists discovered an adult praying mantis preying on small guppies, a type of fish swimming in a pond. To reach the fish, the insect used the floating leaves on the surface of the pond. Of course, the species was the giant rainforest mantis, which is said to be almost 7 centimetres in length.

▲ *The praying mantis has a pair of antennae with which it navigates its surroundings*

Cannibalistic Females

Female praying mantises are interesting insects. To mate, the male has to hop on the female, but if it misses the jump, it becomes the female's next meal. Also, while mating, the female might devour the male's head. The body completes mating after which the rest of the dead male is eaten by the female.

Female praying mantises then lay 12–400 eggs in groups. These are surrounded by a liquid which hardens into a protective shell. The eggs spend the winter protected inside it, to emerge in spring. Infants need the entire summer to grow into adulthood. In case of infants too, many a time their first meal consists of their siblings. Otherwise their meal is fruit flies and very tiny insects.

▼ *A praying mantis sits on a leaf. Observe its front legs and compare it to its hindlegs*

Isn't It Amazing!

Praying mantises are associated with various religious and medicinal beliefs. In Greek they are known as 'mantes', which means prophet. In China, it is thought that these insects help in the cure of goitre, a **thyroid** problem. The Chinese believe that eating roasted eggshells of praying mantises prevents children from wetting their beds at night. These instances reflect how the insect features in various cultures.

ANIMALS | INSECTS

The Hidden Sticks

Stick insects display some of the best camouflage in the world. They resemble twigs. Coincidentally, they also live amongst twigs, making them hard to spot. These insects come in varied sizes. Among the smallest is the 1.30-centimetre-long *Timema cristinae* of North America. Among the biggest is the 38.2-centimetre-long *Phryganistria chinensis* of Sichuan, China. With legs stretched, this insect measures a length of 64 centimetres, making it the longest insect in the world.

A Stick Story

Stick insects are usually green or brown in colour. Many have wings and few have spines. These spines are used in defence to prevent predator attacks. Some play dead to keep the attacker at bay, while few prefer to lose a leg in escape. Additionally, there is one species in North America which releases a foul-smelling liquid. These are nocturnal insects that spend their day motionless amongst plants.

Stick insects are commonly found in the tropics; however, few species also live in the temperate zones. They live in forests and grasslands, where they find ample vegetation to feed on.

▲ Stick insects can regenerate their limbs

Howe a Stick Survived

Lord Howe Island stick insects are big (almost 15 centimetres long), flightless, nocturnal insects named after an island of the same name in the Pacific Ocean. They were first found on this island off the coast of Australia. They are usually blackish or dark brown in colour with a distinct abdomen and six long legs. Their size and appearance have given them nicknames such as land lobster and tree lobster. The young ones of these stick insects are called nymphs and they are green in colour.

◀ *Ctenomorpha gargantua* stick insects are bred in captivity to keep the species intact

Mysterious Appearance

Lord Howe Island stick insects were once so abundant that fishermen used them as bait. A shipwreck and accidental introduction of rats on the island in 1918 wiped out the population of stick insects there. In the 1960s, these stick insects were thought to be extinct. But in 2001, as a miracle, they were found once again about 20 kilometres away from the island on a volcanic remnant called the Ball's Pyramid. How these flightless creatures reached there is a mystery.

These fall in the critically endangered list of the IUCN. Today it is said that only 30–40 survive in the wild. Fortunately, the Australian government is taking strict measures to safeguard and increase the remaining population.

In Real Life

Leaf insects belong to the same order as the stick insects, the order Phasmatodea. They are often called walking leaves because of their uncanny resemblance to a leaf. Many even have a vein structure similar to the leaves. The camouflage nature has created for them is simply stunning! These flat insects feed on plants and are found in the Indian Ocean, Southeast Asia, as well as Australia.

▶ A leaf insect rocks back and forth to mimic a real leaf being blown by the wind

A Historical Pest

Locusts and grasshoppers are cousins. A locust may look as harmless as its cousin on a bright summer morning, as it jumps plant to plant. But do you know a locust can be one of the most devastating insects on the planet?

▲ *Each locust can eat its weight in plants each day*

Appearance

Similar to grasshoppers, locusts are green or tan in colour and have strong hindlegs which allow them to make strong jumps. They make a distinctive noise by rubbing their hindlegs together. They too have external mouthparts. They use their strong, toothed mandibles to cut and chew vegetation. The cut food is held and pushed up into the mouth with the help of pincer-like maxillae. A solitary locust leads a peaceful life. It is a shy creature.

Swarm Formation

Then there could come a phase, wherein the five-centimetre small locust undergoes a complete character change just like Dr Jekyll transforms into Mr Hyde. The locust can turn from good and peaceful to annoyed and vengeful. The most infamous of all species is the desert locust. They live in the desert areas between India and West Africa.

Especially after good rains, where there is a bounty of food, the desert locusts breed. As long as there is enough food for the entire population, the insects are happy. But the moment there is competition, the character of the insect changes. It enters into what is called the gregarious phase. Not just its behaviour, which becomes aggressive, its appearance too changes; it turns black and yellow. The insect is ready to swarm!

A Long March

Desert-locust nymphs (young ones) will move about 300 metres daily to find food, but adult swarms can fly as much as 3,200 kilometres in one year, destroying vegetation along the way. Locusts usually migrate towards low pressure zones where rains are likely. In other words, they follow the rain patterns in the area they live in.

In Real Life

An adult locust can eat vegetation which equals its body weight. Take a guess at how much a small swarm of locusts can eat. It can eat enough food for 2,500 people. It can devastate entire fields within minutes. Swarms are capable of impacting the livelihoods of one-tenth of the people on the planet. In 2004, a swarm of locusts swept across Mauritania to Egypt and went further to Israel in the east and Portugal in the north. Of course, human beings are better equipped today to deal with the swarms than they were in the last century, thanks to improved monitoring and control techniques. But if the infestation goes undetected, it could be years before things are rectified at a cost of millions of dollars.

▲ *Locust swarms can vary from less than one square kilometre to several hundred square kilometres*

▲ *Locusts have affected crops and farmlands since biblical times, attacking any grown green vegetation in their path*

Unwelcome House Guests

External parasites are called ectoparasites. These ectoparasites mostly belong to the insect family. For a parasite living outside the host, the main problem is how to benefit from the host. It either has to stay attached or attach briefly to penetrate the host, at least while it is feeding. The hairy surfaces of mammals are accommodating of many an ectoparasite. A great example is the cat flea.

A Purry Foe

Fleas are small, wingless insects bearing many bristles and spines. Cat fleas are generally host specific, but are found on other animals such as dogs, leopards, civets, and foxes too, if the regular host is not available.

The cat flea has a compressed body that helps it move with ease along cats' fur. The mouthparts are specialised to suck blood while the hindlimbs are developed for jumping on and off the host. It has well-developed knee and hip joints. So it can jump vast distances, equivalent to a man jumping a multi-storey building. The hair on the body and legs stop the flea from falling off the cat's fur. The insect is known to survive on the cat's blood. It causes intense itching and inflammation on the cat's skin.

▲ *A cat flea can sometimes bite human beings if it is not getting enough food from its host*

A Wakeup Bite

Bedbugs are small insects with the appearance of an apple seed. They have flat, rust-coloured bodies. The adults are less than one centimetre long. These insects do not fly, but they can quickly crawl on surfaces. Their mouths are equipped to suck blood.

During the daytime, bedbugs are inactive, but at night they find human beings and suck on their blood. They feed for about 3–10 minutes. Their bodies swell and become bright red. Do you know these bugs can go without food for weeks at a stretch? At right temperatures, based on the availability of food, female bedbugs can lay close to 200–400 eggs.

Bedbugs do not kill human beings, but they lead to itching and red rashes on the skin. The infestation is commonly seen in the crevices of walls, furniture and of course, beds and mattresses, which is where they get their name from.

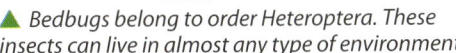
▲ *Bedbugs belong to order Heteroptera. These insects can live in almost any type of environment*

Sleeping Sickness

The tsetse fly, also known as the tik-tik fly, is a bloodsucking fly native to Africa. This yellowish brown or dark brown insect belongs to the housefly family. There are two distinguishing characteristics of the tsetse flies. One is the presence of a piercing, stiff mouthpart that can puncture skin. This is horizontal most times, but it becomes vertical when the insect wants tobite. The second is a bristle-like appendage on each antenna, which bears on its upper edge a row of long, branched hair.

Tsetse flies are known to suck the blood of human beings, as well as domestic and wild animals. In human beings, they cause a disease called sleeping sickness. It leads to muscle aches and fever. The infected person feels tired all the time. If the disease is not treated, it can enter the brain, leading to complications and difficulties in the treatment and cure.

▲ *Tsetse flies are between 6–16 millimetres in length*

The Busy Bee

There exist close to 20,000 species of bees in the world. The Australian *Euryglossina* is just two millimetres long, while the Indonesian *Megachile* is almost four centimetres in length. The world of bees is diverse and colourful. The American sweat bee, attracted to perspiration, is green and blue. On the other hand, the valley carpenter bees have black-bodied females and yellow-bodied males.

Hive Building

Bees live in nests called hives. The central feature of the nest is the cell, a single structure in which the laid egg develops into the pupa. Only in social species, such as the honeybees, are these cells grouped together to form honeycombs, which are made of wax. In these cells, there are areas designated to bring up the young ones and store honey and pollen. Each cell is hexagonal.

Social Structure

In case of a solitary bee, nest-building is carried out by the mother with materials such as soil or wax, but in social bees, the hives are a very organised structure. Honeybee societies are perfectly organised with each 'caste', as it is called, performing its own task. Their tasks consist of three ranks—the smallest and most numerous are the worker bees. These are **sterile** females. Their main function is to build, maintain, and defend the nest.

The worker bees are all females, but do not lay eggs. Also, it is the worker bee which performs the famous dance of the bees, the 'waggle dance'. After a brief flight outside, when a worker bee returns to the hive, it dances to convey the direction in which food sources can be found in plenty.

Eggs are always laid by the queen bee. It is the largest bee in the entire hive and mother to all the workers. Finally, there is the drone bee, whose work is to mate with the queen bee to produce the next generation.

 ▲ One bee colony can produce up to 150 kg of honey per year

💡 Isn't It Amazing!

A honeybee can fly at a speed of 25 kmph and beat its wings almost 200 times per minute. Also, honeybees have close to 170 odour receptors, indicating that smell is important to them. Honeybees use this power to communicate and locate different flowers for food. They also help pollinate the flowers, helping in the process of reproduction by cross-pollination.

 ## The Wax Factory

Wax is produced from the glands on the underside of the worker bees. The bee kneads the wax with its front legs and mouthparts, mixing it with its saliva to make it useable. What is interesting is the temperature of the nest, which is maintained at 45° C to keep the wax soft to work with. Along with the wax, the bees also produce a glue called propolis. It helps in plugging the gaps and cracks in the hive.

▲ The hexagonal cells of the honeycomb have intrigued people since ancient times. It is an efficient shape that is also used by other insects such as the paper wasp

▶ Most bees live a solitary existence. It is only a few such as the honeybees and bumblebees which lead a social life. In their colonies, they do not just live together but work together as well

The Hive

There exist some honeybee hives that contain as many as 100,000 bees. The honeybee hives consist of a number of wax combs suspended from a structure like a tree or a wall. The cells at the borders of the hive contain nectar mixed with saliva. The workers fan this mixture to evaporate the water. The cells are then capped with wax and sealed. This mixture gradually turns into honey. Other cells are used to store pollen. Developing larvae in uncapped cells are looked after by the worker bees. They are fed honey and pollen. On becoming young adults, the bees emerge from the cells, which are cleaned by the worker bees for reuse. The queen lays eggs in the centre of the hive. Drones do not perform any household duties and are driven away in times of food scarcity.

Queen Bee

If the queen bee dies, the workers select a larva and feed it with what is called the 'royal jelly', a nutritious secretion. The larva then develops into the queen bee. She can live for up to 5 years and in summers can lay almost 2,500 eggs per day. She is vital to the functioning of the hive as it is she who directs the work and behaviour of the other bees, and maintains balance in the hive by allocating roles. She communicates all this through chemicals called pheromones, which dictate the behaviour of the bees.

Mistaken Identity

Wasps are close cousins of the bees. They look so similar that it is often a case of mistaken identity. But there are differences between the two insects. Honeybees have a light coat of hair which allows them to trap pollen. Wasps have little to no hair. While honeybees have rounded bodies, wasps have pointed bodies. Honeybees eat nectar, but wasps also eat larval secretions and other insects. Honeybees do not sting people unless they are threatened, but wasps often use their sting as the first defence. Another major difference is that the legs of a honeybee are hidden while flying, but wasps have their legs hanging out while flying.

▲ Closely observe the bodies of the bees to understand their colour patterns ;Honey bee (left) and Yellow jacket wasp (right)

The Useful Bee

The honeybee is one of the most useful insects out there. Apart from giving honey and beeswax to human beings, honeybees pollinate our crops. Pollination is the process of transfer of pollen from the anther of one flower to the stigma of another flower for fertilisation. On pollination, crops produce fruits and seeds.

Threatened Bees

A queen bee lives for about two to five years on an average, but recent trends show diminished longevity too. Also, colonies of honeybees are disappearing rapidly. The European honeybee is affected by 'colony collapse disorder', a condition characterised by the sudden death of colonies. The cause for the same remains a mystery.

Changes in the world of bees can drastically affect humans as well. One example of such change is the bee orchid pollinated by honeybees. Sadly, the plant is being forced to resort to self-pollination. The anther droops forward to contact the stigma of the same flower. This is common in the bee orchids in the far northern reaches of the planet; this has happened because the local population of honeybees there has almost become extinct.

▲ One-third of the world's agricultural crop production depends on pollination

Human Intervention

Honeybees are already reared commercially, but now their dwindling numbers demand our urgent attention. In places where the bee population has dropped down, farmers are resorting to hiring the services of beekeepers. How is this done?

A stack of hives is delivered to a farmer by a beekeeper. The keeper then releases the honeybees on the farm. The bees head towards the plants and begin the process of pollination.

In Real Life

The Asian giant hornets are huge wasps, as big as 5 centimetres long. Their sting is said to be very painful, and their swarms can decimate a beehive in a short time, killing all the bees inside. They then feast on the pupae and larvae. Their sting is fatal even to humans.

Beeswax

Beeswax is used to make candles, artificial fruits and flowers, furniture and floor wax, waxed paper, as well as cosmetics.

The Bumblebee

Bumblebees, also from the bee family, are fat and furry. They are found almost all over the world, except Antarctica. These bees are excellent pollinators. A single bee can visit close to 200 flowers in one trip to eat nectar, each time picking up and leaving behind a bit of the pollen. There are two types of bumblebees—those that build nests and those that are parasitic. There are several species of bumblebees that exist within these types. The average bumblebee is 1.5–2.5 cm in length.

◀ Bumblebees scent-mark the flowers that they have visited

Isn't it Amazing!

Plants do not release their entire nectar in one go. They release it in small amounts, encouraging bees to move from plant to plant, thereby aiding better pollination.

The Silk Road

There is a legend that says that around 3,000 years ago, the wife of Emperor Huangdi came across some threads. She decided to find the source of these threads, as she loved their texture. On searching for the source, she saw that worms living on white mulberry trees were producing the threads. She used the loom to produce lots of silk materials. However, this story might just be a myth. The origins of silk can certainly be traced back to China, but the exact details of this significant discovery are lost in the annals of history.

The Creator

Silk is produced by silkworms. But silkworms are not actually worms, as the name suggests. Instead, they are caterpillars of the silkworm moth. The silkworm caterpillar weaves threads around itself to form a cocoon as protection while it transforms to a moth during its pupa stage.

The silkworm moth has a wingspan that is about 5 centimetres long. It can have wings that look white or light brown in colour. The female silkworm moth is larger than the male. The sad part about these moths is that they live only for a few days. They do not eat in their lifetimes, as their mouthparts are either absent or reduced. They cannot fly either.

▲ A silk moth lays up to 300 eggs at a time

The Real Producer

Female silkworm moths produce about 300–500 eggs which hatch anytime between one to two weeks. The hatched larvae are less than one centimetre long. As soon as they are born, they start feeding on mulberry leaves, their preferred meal. They grow almost up to 7–8 centimetres long in 45 days. The cocoon they weave is of a continuous silk thread, either white or cream in colour, anywhere from 300–900 metres long.

▶ Silkworms only eat mulberry leaves

▲ China is the the world's largest silk producer

 The Martyrs

Sericulture is the process of rearing silkworms and thereafter producing silk. So much domestication has taken place that there are almost no silkworm moths left in the wild anymore. Sadly, to create the shimmering, soft silk that humans love donning, caterpillars have to give up their lives. The first step in the production is to kill the pupae with steam or hot air. People for Ethical Treatment of Animals (PETA) and many other animal organisations have been protesting silk production for some time, but widespread use continues across the world. Silkworms have been **genetically modified** to create tougher and more elastic silk than that of the naturally domesticated variety. After silk threads are collected from the silkworm, they are spun and woven to create silk fabric.

The Builder Ants

Ants are insects that perhaps most human beings are familiar with. There are more than 12,000 species of these insects that exist today. They belong to the same insect order as wasps and bees—Hymenoptera.

The Slim One

Ants have a large head, elbowed antennae, and two sets of jaws; the front one to dig and carry food and the posterior one to chew the food. Ants are small, not more than 3 centimetres long. They come in varied colours, such as brown, red, yellow, and black.

Ants are known to 'hear' with their feet; the feet pick up the ground vibrations. Some such as driver ants have no eyes. In this case, they use their antennae to communicate. Also, they use chemical signals or pheromones to attract mates, warn others of danger, or convey the location of a food source. Ants eat nectar, seeds, fungus, and small insects.

Building a Society

Ant colonies come in varied sizes; they can range from a dozen individuals to a whopping one million of them living together. Similar to the bees, the ants show a structured society with each individual having a job based on its 'caste'.

The ant colony could have one or more queens. The queen lays eggs to create more and more members in the colony. The colony is teeming with worker ants, that are sterile females. There may be more than one type of worker, each performing a specific task. The young workers attend to the queen and look after the eggs and the smallest larvae. The middle-aged workers tend to the larger larvae and pupae, while the oldest of the workers guard the nest and hunt for food. The colony also has soldier ants with large heads and strong jaws for defending the colony.

▲ Armies of ants are known to attack and prey on reptiles, small birds, and even small mammals

Starting a Colony

A colony of ants has males too. At a certain time of the year, male ants and new queens are produced. These are winged adults, unlike the wingless workers. When the environmental conditions are right, the males and the queen leave the nest in a swarm. All ant nests in the area will swarm at the same time to ensure that ants from different parents mate. On mating, the male ants die, while the queens find a suitable nest; once inside, she pulls off her wings, lays eggs, and tends to the brood. When the workers emerge, the nest building begins.

▶ Ants can be found on every single continent except Antarctica

Builders

Ants build nests in varied ways. Some use their jaws to shovel soil around the nest to form volcano-like craters. Some build mounds which they cover with loose vegetation; these mounds help regulate the temperature within the nests. An interesting feature of ants is that the nests are not temperature controlled; the insects move the eggs, larvae, and even themselves to where the temperature is suitable within the nest.

Not all ant nests are underground. In tropical regions, some ants are seen building their nests on trees. These nests are built with paper-like substances made with soil or wood and glued together with sugar solutions produced by ants.

▲ The largest ant nest ever found is over 3,700 miles wide

Traits and Behaviours

Harvester ants often live in areas which are drought prone. To ensure supply of food in times of scarcity, they build vast underground storage areas where seeds are dried and kept. Tailor ants (also known as weaver ants) live on trees and as the name suggests they sew their nests. Large workers fold a leaf with their jaws and feet.

The European garden ant nests in rotting tree logs, under stones, or in loose earth. The main nest is underground and is made up of a series of chambers. When the Sun warms one part of the nest, the eggs and larvae are carried to that part. In winter, the entire colony transfers itself to the interior of the nest.

The Leafcutter ants, on the other hand, feed on fungi, which they culture inside their chambers. How do they do it? The ants cut pieces of leaves and carry them inside the nest. The leaves are chewed upon to help fungus grow on them. This is then eaten by the Leafcutter ants.

In Real Life

Do not disturb the colony of North America's red imported fire ants. They sting so hard that one needs to visit a doctor to get relief. Also, the ants cause a lot of damage to crops. This is not an insect one feels happy to have around!

Usefulness

Ants play an important role in recycling nutrients in an ecosystem. They do so by feeding on and breaking down small animals, other invertebrates, and plants. In the process of building homes, they 'till' the soil, which means they bring up the deeper layers of soil to the surface. These layers, with nutrients intact, are used by plants for growth.

Ants feed on the eggs of other insects but also, they are prey for lizards and birds. The tunnels they build aerate the surrounding soil. In fact, all of this digging helps them store the seeds that fall off of fruits and other plants. But ants can also cause damage. If their population is left unchecked, they can also destroy plants.

▲ Ants have superhuman strength! They can carry 10–50 times their body weight!

◀ Ants hold the record for the fastest movement in the animal kingdom

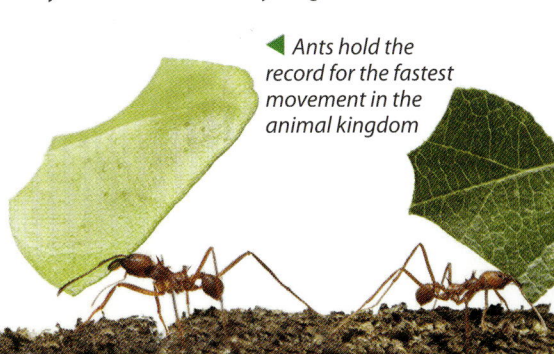

The Active Termites

Termites, another set of social insects, are found mainly in the warmer parts of the world. They are **xylophages**, which basically means that they are wood-eaters. Termites are known to damage thousands of trees every year. But they are also quite useful. Termites play an important role in decomposing plants and breaking down nutrients. They can do so because they have bacteria in their stomach which allow them to digest wood. These soft-bodied insects, unlike ants, do not have a waist. Their antennae are a series of segments. Many species of this small, pale insect are completely blind. There are around 2,000 species of termites in existence in this world.

▲ Termite mounds can be up to 30 ft high!

A Model Home

Termite nests vary in size and shape. Some rise like castles above the ground, complete with chimney-like turrets, while others hang from trees. *Cubitermes* have mushroom-shaped homes, while another species, the *Thoracotermes* have straight pillar-like homes.

▲ An arboreal termite nest. These nests are brown and have little bumps on the outside

Building Material

The main building materials in several species of termites that build big homes are soil and saliva. The second type of building material is carton, made up of a mixture of saliva and faecal remains and is used to build walls within the nest.

Mounds of termites are a common site in the African savannah. One species found there is the *Macrotermes natalensis*. These termites are capable of building homes with arches, an incredible feat of architecture for such a small insect. These arches provide a good air-conditioning system inside the nest. This type of nest has close to 2 million termites at one time and could take years to be built.

Termite nests need to accommodate a large number of insects living together, and it is for this reason that their mounds can reach heights of 17 feet and higher. The average termite mound can have around 15 kilograms of termites. In a typical year, these insects move almost 250 kilograms of soil and several tons of water.

▶ Termites have been nicknamed 'silent destructors' by human beings because they can eat through paper and wood in a person's house without detection

Isn't It Amazing!

Neocapritermes taracua are termites found in South America. They have an interesting defence mechanism. The aged workers of the colony grow sacs which are filled with a toxic, blue liquid. When they feel that the colony is threatened or a predator approaches, these sacs explode. They sacrifice their lives for the nest.

The Home Makers

In contrast to bees and ants, termite colonies contain an equal number of males and females, most of which are sterile. These are further divided into two categories; the regular workers and the soldiers. The soldiers do not look for food. They are fed **regurgitated** food; instead their duty is to guard the nest.

The workers are divided into two parts. The bigger ones are sent to forage for food, while the smaller ones build and repair the nest, look after the young ones, other members, as well as the royal couple.

There is usually a single royal couple in the colony. The king or the male is not as large as the queen or the female. The queen's abdomen increases dramatically in size during the egg-laying stage. The queen can lay as many as 30,000 eggs per day. The young ones born are a part of the same colony.

▲ Termite and ant colonies sometimes go to war over territory and access to food

New Homes

Every termite colony has alates—temporarily winged males and females. A new termite colony is set up by the alates. The male is attracted to the female by an odour produced by the female; she has a gland meant for this on the underside of her belly. When the weather conditions are conducive, the alates swarm. Similar to ants, colonies of the same termite species in the area swarm at the same time, allowing breeding between individuals born to different parents. The temporary wings help young adults take flight; they then find their mates. Once on the ground, they shed their wings, build a small nest and seal themselves inside to mate and start a new colony.

Termites use different materials to build their homes. They mark all their construction materials with chemicals that they themselves produce. These chemicals dissolve over time. New chambers can emerge from the tunnels that they build in their homes. As the chemicals dissolve, termites can even make out if the chambers are old or new.

▲ Termite queens have the longest lifespan of any insect in the world: 25–50 years!

The Fungal Story

Macrotermes natalensis is a fungus-growing termite species commonly found in South Africa. These termites prefer dead plant material which has been made soft by fungus. In the dry season, the food supply diminishes as fungus needs humid conditions to thrive. To avoid this situation, the termites create fungus chambers with the help of carton. The fungus grows well in the humid atmosphere of the nest, giving enough food to the insects. Few of the termites from this species dig deeper to find water, so that it provides humid conditions for the fungus to thrive.

Incredible Individuals

We know a lot about termites and their homes because of scientists. In fact, a group of scientists once prepared 500 different termite nests. These were simulated nests. They compared them to real termite nests and found that termites design everything of value within close distances. This is to ensure fast transportation. A scientist named J. Scott Turner experimented with termite nests or termite mounds by filling them with propane, stuffing them with plaster and scanning them with lasers. He even fed the termites microscopic beads and gave them fluorescent green water. He did all this to figure out how termites built their massive nests.

The Dangerous Mosquito

If you have ever sat outside on a summer evening, especially in the tropics, you will be familiar with this little pest. They create small red spots where they bite, and you are left scratching the spot. They don't just attack in the evenings, mosquitoes can be a menace at any time of the day. They do not just bite, but can also cause death, though not directly. Just three species of this insect are enough to wreak havoc on humans.

Bite

The body of a mosquito, when feeding, swells to such an extent that its skin stretches and becomes transparent enough for us to see the human blood inside. The mosquito's mouthparts are adapted for piercing the human skin. They consist of four **stylets** to pierce the skin. While biting, they stab two tubes into the victim. One is to pump in anti-coagulants which prevent the victim's blood from clotting and another is from which the blood is sucked.

Mosquitoes use a few signals to spot their victims, such as exhaled carbon dioxide, body odours, and even movement. Both male and female mosquitoes eat nectar and other sugars from plants. It is only the females which bite, since they use it as a source of protein to lay eggs.

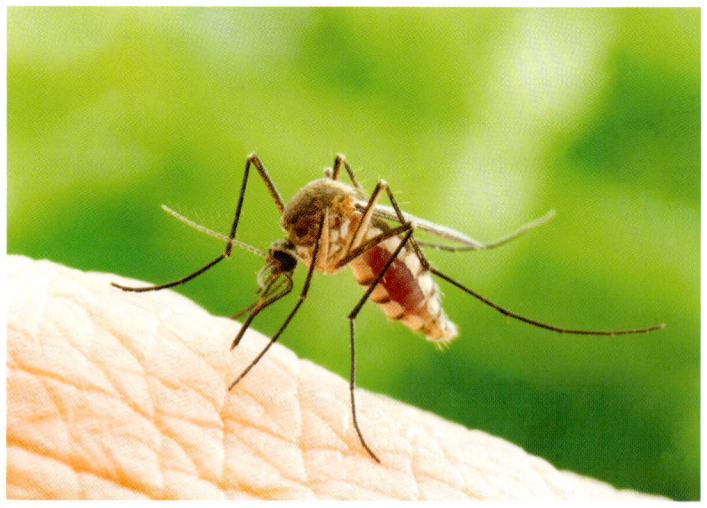
▲ Mosquito bites can cause many diseases, such as malaria, dengue, etc.

The Deadly Threesome

Mosquito-borne diseases are so prevalent that they are amongst the first priority of the World Health Organisation (WHO) as well as governments of countries affected. The deadliest are the following three types—the Anopheles, which is known to cause malaria as well as transmit filariasis and encephalitis; the Aedes, which spreads dengue, yellow fever, and encephalitis; and lastly the Culex, which causes filariasis, encephalitis as well as West Nile virus.

Prevention

It is possible to control the spread of such diseases by controlling the vector. One important method is to destroy the mosquito in its larval stage itself. Mosquitoes need water to breed; especially if the water is stagnant, the larvae breed undisturbed. Careful monitoring of such sites has helped control the menace to a great extent in many African and Southeast Asian countries. Another method is to kill adult mosquitoes using insecticides.

Vector

Did you know that the mosquito does not inherently have such disease-causing abilities? It is merely the vector, in other words carrier, of microorganisms which cause these diseases. In case of malaria, the plasmodium parasite attaches itself to the gut of the female mosquito. The moment the mosquito stings the victim for blood, it releases itself into the blood of the victim. Similarly, in dengue and yellow fever, the mosquito is the carrier of viruses that cause the diseases.

▲ Mosquitoes have a nerve that indicates when the stomach is filled; otherwise it would not stop drinking and burst from the pressure

Incredible Individuals

Charles Louis Alphonse Laveran (1845–1922) was a French doctor who found out the causal agent of malaria. While serving in Algeria, he was troubled by the outbreak of malaria in the army. While others blamed bad air ('*mala aria*' in Italian), he followed Louis Pasteur's line of thought which dictated that most infectious diseases are a result of germs. By 1880, he had enough evidence to prove that malaria was caused by mosquitoes won the Nobel Prize in Physiology or Medicine in 1907

▲ Charles Louis Alphonse Laveran

The Irksome Housefly

Houseflies are a regular feature of our world. There are over 110,000 species of flies, out of which houseflies are just one. They live in almost all environments, except Antarctica.

Distribution

Houseflies are attracted to a range of things including water, exposed food particles, garbage as well as carrion. The latter two, garbage, and carrion, are certainly full of many infectious microorganisms; when the fly sits on them, its feet pick them up. Now, if the fly's next stop is exposed food, it transfers the microorganisms to the food. Once human beings consume this food, it leads to a variety of diseases such as cholera, diarrhoea, and typhoid.

A Fly's Body

Houseflies are dull grey in colour with yellowish areas on the abdomen and grey stripes on the thorax. They are less than 1 centimetre long. What is interesting is that the housefly uses only one pair of wings in flight. This is because the second pair is reduced to knob-like structures called halters. It is these that help the housefly maintain balance while flying. Houseflies have huge compound eyes, which give them better vision.

Upside Down

At the end of the housefly's feet there are sharp claws and lots of sticky hair. This is because of the secretions produced by small glandular pads present between each claw on the feet. The claws and feet help the housefly hold onto surfaces when it is upside down. Also, being light in weight helps their bodies to hold on without falling.

The Egg Story

A female housefly deposits close to 100 eggs at one time. In her lifespan she can produce up to 1,000 eggs. The eggs hatch anytime in the span of 24 hours. The housefly eggs undergo complete metamorphosis, which means they go from being larva to pupa to an adult. A housefly can live for a month or two.

▲ *Houseflies rely on their sense of smell when they source for food*

▲ *Houseflies' amazing eyes allow them to see behind them*

Sponge-like Mouths

The short feelers of houseflies act like their nose. Once they pick up the smell of an object, they fly towards it. They use their feet hair to find out how something tastes. If they like it, their sponge-like mouthparts lap it up. Due to the soft mouthparts, a housefly cannot bite.

💡 Isn't It Amazing!

The fruit fly (*Drosophila melanogaster*) is the most-studied multicellular creature in the world. Thomas Hunt Morgan (1866–1945) chose it as a 'model organism' for research in genetics—the study of genes. Fruit flies have a lifecycle of 10 days, and can be grown in glass bottles. By studying thousands of mutant flies, we have learnt a lot about how our genes guide our development.

▲ *Houseflies "mostly breed on trash cans, animal dung, human excrement, decaying vegetable, and animal materials*

Word Check

Arthropods: They form the largest order of the animal kingdom, mainly consisting of animals with 'jointed' legs.

Bioluminescence: It is the process by which light is emitted from a living organism like a glow-worm or firefly.

Cross pollinators: It refers to sources of pollination of a flower or plant with pollen from another flower or plant.

Defoliation: It is the destruction of leaves.

Ectoparasites: These are parasites that live outside the body of the host.

Elytra: They are the hardened wings of an insect like a beetle or weevil.

Genetically modified: It refers to the process of altering the genetic constituency. Both organisms as well as fruits and vegetables can be genetically modified.

Hibernate: It means to spend days in a state of inactivity, especially during winters when sources of food are minimum, and the weather is not conducive for survival.

Incomplete metamorphosis: Similar to metamorphosis, but here the pupa stage is absent

Metamorphosis: It is the process by which an organism transforms from its younger stage to an adult. After this transformation, the adult does not resemble the young ones from the same species.

Monophagous: It refers to feeding on a single kind of plant or animal.

Moulting: It is the process by which an animal sheds its exoskeleton to regrow a new one.

Nymph: It is the form of an insect that does not transform in appearance as it grows.

Parasitic: It is the practice or behaviour of an organism that depends on exploiting another organism for survival.

Regurgitated: It refers to food that is swallowed by animals and then brought up again.

Sericulture: It is the process of rearing silkworms and thereafter producing silk.

Spiracles: The small openings or holes on the exoskeleton that allow an animal to breathe.

Sterile: It refers to an organism that is unable to reproduce.

Stridulating: It means to produce a sharp and shrill sound by rubbing the wings, legs or other body parts together.

Stylets: Thin and needle-like insect mouthparts.

Thyroid: It is a small gland which regulates the growth and development of the body.

Xylophage: It refers to an insect or organism that feeds on wood.